ELEV8 yourlife.love

THE ESSENTIALS WORKBOOK

THE ESSENTIALS WORKBOOK

SUNNY DAWN JOHNSTON

 PRODUCTIONS

ELEV8 Your Life
The Essentials Workbook

Copyright © 2018
By Sunny Dawn Johnston

Cover Design and Logos by Graphic Designer Kris Voelker
Interior Graphics by Staci Lee Randall
Interior Design by Deb McGowan
Formatted for Print by Shanda Trofe

For permission requests, write to the publisher:
SDJ Productions
4640 W. Redfield Road
Glendale, AZ 85306
www.sdjproductions.net

ISBN-13: 978-1-7324357-0-4

Printed in the United States of America.

Dedicated to those who are inspired to ELEVATE their life.

CONTENTS

The Journey to ELEV8 Your Life

ELEV8YourLife.love is your complete roadmap to living a more high vibe, authentic, joyful life.

This roadmap breaks down the progression of healing into 5 key steps: *I'm Feelin' the Pain, Eyes Wide Open, Ch Ch Ch Choices, Lights!!! Camera!!! Action!!! and I'm Feelin' the Healin'.*

Best of all, each area has its own set of characteristics that help you determine which step you're in, what areas to focus on, what emotions you can expect and a set of benchmarks to reach before you move onto the next step.

The entire goal of this roadmap is to eliminate your overwhelm, keep you focused and moving towards a more joyful, happy life.

So how did I come up with this roadmap? To explain, I need to take you back to the beginning. My name is Sunny Dawn, and, yes, "Sunny Dawn" is my birth name. That is the first question I am often asked when someone meets me for the first time or hears my name. My birth name is the perfect vibration for me, and my mother knew that when she picked it out when she was fifteen. My mom only had to wait another six years for my grand entrance into the physical world, and, oh boy, was it grand!

I was raised in Utah, so the second most common question I am asked is, "Are you Mormon?" I spent ten years of my childhood growing up in Salt Lake City, and when people hear that, they naturally assume I am Mormon. Well the answer to that question is no, I am not Mormon. My religion is simply Love! When I was three years old and living in the Philippines, I witnessed extreme abuse in the name of religion, and that experience changed my perception of religion. I would say that I am "spiritual" rather than religious, as spirituality more closely aligns with my vibration. Not to say that I am against any religion. I believe that religion serves many; I simply don't identify with religion for myself.

At age thirteen, I had my first angelic experience; I saw my first Angel. I was surprised when I awoke to a brilliant, glowing, angelic being hovering above my bed. But I wasn't afraid, because the peaceful energy that emanated from this glow felt like pure love. I soaked it up and felt calm, serene, and supported as I drifted back to sleep. This was my first experience with the angelic realm, and I continued to have many more throughout my life. Even though each experience was different, the energy of absolute unconditional love was the same. Regardless of what was going on in my life, the angelic realm was always present. Sometimes I chose to listen, other times not. I denied, resisted, and even ignored them, yet they still remained. This is the unconditional love that is available to each and every one of you, every moment of your life.

I am a lifelong student. Perhaps you are too? The last thirty-four years have been an amazing journey for me, and each day I experience divine intervention in the form of Angels, Archangels, Spirit Guides, Ascended Masters, and the beautiful physical bodies that walk this planet with me.

I've learned many things through this journey:
- I am responsible for my life.
- I've created my challenges by my own resistance to love.
- I was born with innate value, simply because I was born into a physical body.
- I did not need to earn, prove, or justify my worth.
- I am worthy because I am.

I've forgotten these simple but true statements many times in my life. Perhaps you have too? There was no one to blame and nothing at fault. It was part of my path, a very important part of my path—maybe the most important! The pain, discomfort, challenge, or lack were all awarenesses that eventually led to my acknowledgment of my own self-worth. The Spirit World has surrounded and guided me while I was given opportunities to see my unique and divine value. The choice to love and accept myself was hard… and yet, it was mine to make, as it is yours.

Throughout this **ELEV8 Your Life** program, I will hold your hand, and be here to support you and walk with you as you move through your own challenges and resistance. I know how it feels to be stuck in the pain… and I KNOW how it feels to be Feelin' the Healin'! **ELEV8 Your Life** is a process … a lifestyle … of looking at the painful or challenging patterns, becoming aware of those messages, choosing a different story, pushing thru to new actions and therefore arriving at a place where you begin to feel the joy and the healing in your Mind, Body and Spirit.
Let's start this journey together, shall we?

So…. Where do you start? Which of the five steps are you (mostly) in? Let's help you find that out.

Step 1: I'm Feelin' the Pain

This is the first step in your roadmap and typically where most of us start out.

You'll know you are in the *I'm Feelin' the Pain* step if:

- You feel like the hurt will never end, and you feel paralyzed and shutdown.
- You feel like a victim, no one cares, or nobody understands.
- You stuff your emotions.

- You blame others, feel powerless, feel like you are being punished, feel afraid, feel stuck.
- You don't feel fulfilled, have a negative outlook, feel like you are going thru the motions, have no reason to go on or don't want to live.
- You don't know how to move forward and feel like the fear is going to take you over.
- You struggle with your weight or fear your body will never be healthy again.

Do you see yourself in that breakdown? If so, you've probably experienced at least one of these emotions:

- Hopeless
- Fearful
- Unhappy
- Angry
- Unfulfilled

Feel familiar ... if so ... you are feeling your pain.

Fortunately, this is also the step where you can feel:

- Excited about the possibilities
- Proud of yourself for becoming aware
- Inspired to have a different life
- Joy at knowing why you feel the way you do

So, what are the things you want to focus on in *I'm Feelin' the Pain*?

Things like:

- Create your own affirmations to use daily
- Meditate for a minimum of 5 minutes
- Journal about your emotional, physical, mental, or spiritual pain for 10 minutes
- Go for a walk, or move your body for 15 minutes
- Invite Archangel Michael in to help maintain your energy everyday

And so much more.

So how do you know when you have moved from a place of Feelin' the Pain into one of Awareness?

Ideally, you can answer yes to the following:

- Do you want to expand your awareness of the mind, body, spirit connection?
- Are you aware that you are carrying pain in your mind, body, spirit or emotions?
- Are you willing to experience joy?
- Are you aware of what your pattern of pain is?

If these feel true for you, then you can move your way into ...

Step 2: Eyes Wide Open

Ahhh yes, your eyes wide open ... or typically referred to as awareness.

Awareness is the step where you begin to recognize the patterns that you continue to engage in and feel that there is something greater than yourself in this world.

You'll know you are in the *Eyes Wide Open* step if:

- You wonder if Spirit might be trying to send a message to you.
- You recognize the judgment of yourself or others.
- You tune into your body and recognize the feelings happening inside.
- You want to learn more.
- You want more out of life.

Do you see yourself in that breakdown? If so, you've probably experienced at least one of these emotions:

- Curious
- Anxious
- Questioning
- Open
- Receptive

Feel familiar ... if so ... you are becoming aware.

Fortunately, this is also the step where you can feel:

- Interested in fulfilling a purpose in this world
- Sensitive to the synchronicities happening for me
- Willing to take responsibility for your life
- Motivated to do something different

So, what are the things you want to focus on in the *Eyes Wide Open* step?

Things like:

- Ask Spirit to show you a sign that they are with you
- Look at your environment around you and list everything you notice in your present space for the next 5 minutes
- Visualize white light coming into your crown to create a Spirit connection so as to become more open to seeing messages and signs
- Pay attention to signs and symbols from Spirit throughout your day: Numbers, letters, words, symbols, songs, etc. Jot down the messages you catch

And so much more.

So how do you know when you have moved from Awareness to Choice?

Ideally, you can answer yes to the following:

- Do you recognize that everything happens for a reason?
- Are you willing to call a truce with your body?
- Are you willing to take personal responsibility for your life?
- Are you willing to do something different?

If these feel true for you, then you can move your way into ...

Step 3: Ch Ch Ch Choices

This is where all the fun begins. You roll up your sleeves and realize that you are the creator of your life and your experiences.

You'll know you are in the *Ch Ch Ch Choices* step if:

- You find yourself thinking "Not one more time, will I _____."
- You know if you don't do something differently, then nothing is going to change.
- You are no longer arguing for your limitations.
- You are asking "What's for my highest good?"

Do you see yourself in that breakdown? If so, you've probably experienced at least one of these emotions:

- Empowered
- Confused
- Responsible

- Pressured
- Determined

Feel familiar ... if so ... you are making choices.

Fortunately, this is also the step where you can feel:

- Freedom
- Excitement at choosing how you want to feel
- Open to receiving support
- Pride for choosing to invest in your health

So, what are the things you want to focus on in *Ch Ch Ch Choices*?

Things like:

- Put yourself at the top of your calendar today and do something joyful for yourself for 1 hour
- Pick one area in your life where you feel like you have no choices, and list all the possible outcomes from that experience – dig deep and really look at all your options
- Share 10 ways in which you argue for your limitations / make excuses for yourself
- Do one thing to improve your health today
- Make a choice to step into a fear today and write about the experience before and afterwards

And so much more.

So how do you know when you have moved from Choice into Action?

Ideally, you can answer yes to the following:

- Are you ready to accept your body as your BFF?
- Can you allow yourself to receive support?
- Are you willing to step out of the fear to release the patterns and create a new story?
- Are you willing to commit to be consistent in a new habit for 21 days?

If these feel true for you, then you can move your way into ...

Step 4: Lights!!! Camera!!! Action!!!

This is where the movement starts picking up steam!

You'll know you are in the *Lights!!! Camera!!! Action!!!* step if:

- You make the shift from knowing to doing.
- You struggle to follow through with your intentions.
- You have a willingness to change.
- You adopt a new health routine.
- You are uneasy participating in new activities that support and nurture you.
- You connect with like-minded people.

Do you see yourself in that breakdown? If so, you've probably experienced at least one of these emotions:

- Scared
- Uncertain
- Eager
- Empowered
- Uncomfortable

Feel familiar ... if so ... you are taking action.

Fortunately, this is also the step where you can feel:

- Excited about changing your belief systems
- Satisfied about following thru with agreements with yourself
- Successful and optimistic
- Upbeat about the possibilities

So, what are the things you want to focus on in *Lights!!! Camera!!! Action!!!*?

Things like:

- Do something you are afraid of today
- After waking up in the morning, thank Spirit for this beautiful day and ask, "How May I Be of Service?" Listen throughout the day for your answer
- Reach out to a person that you know is struggling in a similar way as you have in the past. Share with them your experience and offer them some support, encouragement, or simply an ear to listen
- Ask your angels for inspired action and take it
- Commit to sharing one personal affirmation per day via social media for 11 days

And so much more.

So how do you know when you have moved from Action into Healing?

Ideally, you can answer yes to the following:

- Do you feel in harmony with your mind, body, spirit, and emotions?
- Are you ready to be of service to others?
- Are you willing to walk your talk?
- Are you willing to share your experiences from a place of vulnerability?

If these feel true for you, then you can move your way into ...

Step 5: I'm Feelin' the Healin'

This is where you are making positive changes in your life and building up your feelings of confidence and gratitude!

You'll know you are in the *I'm Feelin' the Healin'* step if:

- You can recognize the value of your experiences.
- You want to engage more and share more with others.
- You know that you are moving forward.
- You are frustrated that setbacks still occur.
- You struggle to set healthy boundaries in your new world and new awareness.

Do you see yourself in that breakdown? If so, you've probably experienced at least one of these emotions:

- Forgiveness
- Frustration
- Peace
- Inspiration
- Empowerment

Feel familiar ... if so ... you are feelin' the healin'!

This is also the step where you can feel:

- Pleased about making positive choices for yourself
- Confident in maintaining your vibration
- Grateful for understanding the purpose of your pain
- Freedom from the need to blame

So, what are the things you want to focus on in *I'm Feelin' the Healin'*

Things like:

- Write a letter of forgiveness (to yourself or someone else) and burn it
- Do something that brings you joy every day for one week
- Write 33 things you appreciate about your past and present
- List 10 things you are inspired by or inspired to do - and pick one to reach out for, engage in, donate to, or take action around
- Share a recent experience where you were able to respond, instead of reacting

And so much more.

So how do you know when you have moved thru the I'm Feelin' the Healin' into the ongoing spiral of expansion and growth in all areas of your life?

Ideally, you can answer yes to the following:

- I live my life joyfully
- I am sharing my authentic self
- I am of service to others
- I am open and willing to receive all the abundance and love that life has to offer

If these feel true for you, then high fives are coming at you!

... AND ...

If you have enjoyed this workbook and are not yet a part of the magic of the ELEV8 community of like-hearted individuals, you're gonna have to join **www.ELEV8YourLife.Love** You will find sooooo many more tools, processes, teachings and life long friends in ELEV8. I sure hope to see you there.

Here's to Elevating ... One step at a time!!!!

~Sunny Dawn Johnston

ELEV8

yourlife.love

I'm Feelin' the Pain

Step 1

STEP 1
I'm Feelin' the Pain

This is the first step in your journey and typically where most of us start out.

You'll know you are in the *I'm Feelin' the Pain* Step if:

- You feel like the hurt will never end, and you feel paralyzed and shutdown
- You feel like a victim, no one cares, or nobody understands
- You stuff your emotions
- You blame others, feel powerless, feel like you are being punished, feel afraid, feel stuck
- You don't feel fulfilled, have a negative outlook, feel like you are going thru the motions, have no reason to go on or don't want to live
- You don't know how to move forward and feel the fear is going to take you over
- You struggle with your weight or fear your body will never be healthy again

Do you see yourself in any of this breakdown?

If so, you've probably experienced at least one of these emotions:

- Hopeless
- Fearful
- Unhappy
- Angry
- Unfulfilled

Feel familiar? If so ... you are feeling your pain.

Let's get started with our Video Lessons for this Step:

1. **You Want Something Different**
2. **What Pain Represents**
3. **What are Your Patterns?**
4. **Are You an Observer, or Absorber?**
5. **Disconnection from Spirit**
6. **You Are Not Alone**
7. **Raising your Vibration**
8. **Start with Intention**

Lesson 1
You Want Something Different

You've been uncomfortable in your comfortableness; or vice versa, comfortable in your uncomfortableness. You want to experience something different.

Key Takeaways

- I'm sick and tired of feeling this way ... whatever that is.
- Pain and conflict can become comfortable. Feeling comfortable is not always healthy.
- Through the pain/challenge, your Spirit is nudging you to do something different.

Points to Ponder

In what way(s) has your pain become too comfortable or uncomfortable?

_____

_____

_____

_____

_____

_____

_____

_____

_____

_____

_____

Lesson 2
What Pain Represents

Pain simply represents the fact that there is something out of alignment with who you really are, whether it is being expressed physically, mentally, emotionally, or spiritually.

Key Takeaways

- You came into this world from Spirit – existing at your core as Unconditional Love.
- When your actions, thoughts, reactions or belief system conflicts with your core of Unconditional Love, it will manifest in your life as pain ... physically, mentally, emotionally, or spiritually.
- Pain in your life is an indicator that you are out of alignment with the core of who you are: Unconditional Love.

Points to Ponder
What is the source of your greatest pain right now?

_____

_____

_____

_____

_____

_____

_____

_____

_____

_____

Lesson 3
What are Your Patterns?

Pain can be a learned pattern. You have been trained by people to react in certain ways. You can retrain yourself. A lack of self-esteem can continue self-sabotaging behaviors.

Key Takeaways

- Your thoughts and reactions have been shaped by the people and environment around you. This is your Subconscious training.
- Your beliefs about your own value will affect your self-esteem and contribute to a pattern of behavior that sabotages your connection to the core of you: Unconditional Love.
- You can retrain yourself to adopt new patterns that pull you back into your alignment with that Unconditional Love at the core. This allows you to move from a Subconscious reaction to a Conscious response.

Points to Ponder
How does your Self-Esteem compare to your Self-Worth?

_____

_____

_____

_____

_____

_____

_____

_____

Lesson 4
Are You an Observer, or Absorber?

Maintain your energy, rather than carry other people's pain around within you. Let go of control.

Key Takeaways

- We each have our own energy field we are responsible for maintaining every day. As you interact with others, you often unconsciously *Absorb* the energy that person may be experiencing.
- Invoking Archangel Michael will help you to maintain and support your own energy.
- By letting go of the attempt to control someone else's experience, you can make the choice to *Observe* their actions and behaviors without absorbing them.

Points to Ponder

List those areas in your life that you tend to absorb, rather than observe, the energy of the situation?

_____

_____

_____

_____

_____

_____

_____

_____

_____

Lesson 5
Disconnection from Spirit

The depth of pain you feel is equal to the amount of disconnection (grief, loss) from your Spirit that you are experiencing.

Key Takeaways

- When you are disconnected from your Spirit, you feel it as loss, aloneness, fear, protection, etc.
- The bigger the gap you are experiencing from your core of Unconditional Love, the greater the pain will feel in your life and in your body.
- Separation and disconnection show us what areas we really need to heal in our lives.

Points to Ponder
I feel the most disconnection from my Spirit in this area:

_____

_____

_____

_____

_____

_____

_____

_____

_____

_____

_____

Lesson 6
You Are Not Alone

Spirit is always with you. Your angels are around you. Your loved ones are there in Spirit as well.

Key Takeaways

- You are assigned a Guardian Angel and a Spirit Guide to walk this human journey with you.
- Even when you feel alone, it is the "feeling" that creates the separation ... They never leave.
- When you feel alone, that is the most important time to go within – instead of outside of yourself – for connection.

Points to Ponder
I feel most alone when _____.

_____

_____

_____

_____

_____

_____

_____

_____

_____

_____

Lesson 7
Raising your Vibration

Joy is the highest expression of love and the quickest way to raise your vibration.

Key Takeaways

- How much time do you spend in JOY a day?
- What is the meaning of JOY and why is it important ... As we raise our vibe, it helps us to connect with Spirit.
- What is Joy to you?

Points to Ponder
List some examples of things that raise the vibe for you:

_____

_____

_____

_____

_____

_____

_____

_____

_____

_____

Lesson 8
Start with Intention

Finding harmony in your life can be challenging. Create your day by adding intention to your morning routine.

Key Takeaways

- How do you spend the first hour of your morning and why is it important?
- The 5 things I do every morning to create an amazing day ... therefore, an amazing life.
- Create your day or it will be created for you (Creating vs. Reacting).

Points to Ponder
What are you willing to do in the first hour of your day to start creating it with intention?

_____

_____

_____

_____

_____

_____

_____

_____

_____

_____

_____

I'm Feelin' the Pain
Homework Action Items

Recognize the Mind-Body-Spirit Connection
- ☐ Be present in your body - Feel the sun … Touch the earth.
- ☐ Meditate for a minimum of 5 minutes.
- ☐ Read an inspirational book, blog, article, etc. to redirect/uplift your energy.

Recognize the Pain
- ☐ Open your arms to the Universe each morning and say: "I am open to receive healing for _____."
- ☐ Create 10 affirmations on sticky notes or notecards to say out loud to yourself daily, especially when you feel your vibration dropping.
- ☐ Write down your fears on a piece of paper: Write FEAR in the center of the page. List all your fears around that center word that come up for you in the next 10 minutes.

Experience Joy
- ☐ Raise your vibration by dancing, listening to music, or singing for 15 minutes.
- ☐ Invite Archangel Michael in to help maintain your energy every day.
- ☐ Write one page of gratitude/appreciations.

Understand the Patterns
- ☐ Put your hand on your heart and ask yourself "What is this pain trying to show me?" Write down what comes to you.
- ☐ Journal about your emotional, physical, mental, spiritual pain for 10 minutes.
- ☐ Use your voice to express your feelings to a safe person/counselor.

REMINDER: These Action Items can be done any time during this Step, in any order you are drawn to … and certainly not all should be completed at once, to allow you an opportunity to fully integrate the new behaviors.

I'm Feelin' the Pain
Affirmations to Move Forward

- ♥ I have an expanded awareness of the Mind, Body, Spirit connection.
- ♥ I am aware of the pain I am carrying in my mind, body, spirit or emotions.
- ♥ I am open to experiencing joy.
- ♥ I am aware of the repeating patterns of pain I have been stuck in.

ELEV8
yourlife.love

Eyes
Wide
Open

Step 2

STEP 2
Eyes Wide Open

This is the second step in your journey. Ahhh yes, your eyes wide open ... or typically referred to as awareness. Awareness is the step where you begin to recognize the patterns that you continue to engage in and feel that there is something greater than yourself in this world.

You'll know you are in the *Eyes Wide Open* step if:

- You wonder if Spirit might be trying to send a message to you
- You recognize the judgment of yourself or others
- You tune into your body and recognize the feelings happening inside
- You want to learn more
- You want more out of life

Do you see yourself in any of this breakdown?

If so, you've probably experienced at least one of these emotions:

- Curious
- Anxious
- Questioning
- Openness
- Receptive

Feel familiar? If so ... you are becoming aware.

Let's get started with our Video Lessons for this Step:

1. **Language of Spirit**
2. **Practice Presence**
3. **Intuitive Messages**
4. **Emotion Manifests in the Body**
5. **Taking Things Personally**
6. **No Mistakes**
7. **Why Me?**
8. **Get Out of Your Head**

Lesson 1
Language of Spirit

Learn how Spirit speaks to you.

Key Takeaways

- Explain how Spirit speaks – analogy of moving to China, need to learn a new language.
- Our physical bodies are dense, and Spirit is light – explain the Vibrational chart.
- The Clairs – What are the Clairs?

Points to Ponder
What signs has Spirit been showing you most recently?

_____

_____

_____

_____

_____

_____

_____

_____

_____

_____

_____

_____

_____

Lesson 2
Practice Presence

Being in the present moment is where your power – and Spirit's messages – can be found.

Key Takeaways

- Where are your thoughts? Keeping them in the present.
- We can't experience our deceased loved one's presence when focused on their absence.
- Spirit speaks in present moment only – never in the past, never in the future.

Points to Ponder
In what area of your life are you the most/least present and what are you willing to do to change that?

_____

_____

_____

_____

_____

_____

_____

_____

_____

_____

_____

_____

_____

Lesson 3
Intuitive Messages

Use the 5 "Clairs" to discern your intuitive messages.

Key Takeaways

- Which is your strongest intuitive skill? Take the Clairs Quiz.
- Intuition is like a muscle – you gotta use it.
- Recognizing synchronicities, signs and symbols from Spirit.
- Practice with a couple of intuitive exercises – colored sheets of paper, cards, etc.

Points to Ponder
What is your strongest "Clair" and how can you develop it even more?

_____

_____

_____

_____

_____

_____

_____

_____

_____

_____

_____

Lesson 4
Emotion Manifests in the Body

Become aware of how emotion manifests in your body and identify how emotions create illness, disease, and pain.

Key Takeaways

- Emotions are just energy too. We are often not taught healthy ways to express emotion.
- By expressing our emotions, we can move (release) energy out of the body.
- Dis-ease in particular spots in the body can be an indicator to the type of emotion that has not been expressed (*You Can Heal Your Life* by Louise Hay; *The Secret Language of the Body* by Inna Segal).

Points to Ponder
How do you feel about the possibility that our emotions manifest in our bodies?

_____

_____

_____

_____

_____

_____

_____

_____

_____

_____

_____

Lesson 5
Taking Things Personally

Don't take things personally – people are just talking to themselves: *"Your opinion of me is none of my business."*

Key Takeaways

- You can only identify something in someone else if you have it within yourself – Shadow side.
- Discern when your reaction to someone else is triggering a past pain for you – that part is about you.
- Letting go of comparison – shared the *Comparison* poem.

Points to Ponder
When was the last time you took something personally? Can you look into that a bit more and see how it really isn't about you?

_____

_____

_____

_____

_____

_____

_____

_____

_____

_____

Lesson 6
No Mistakes

Everything happens for a reason; there truly are no mistakes.

Key Takeaways

- If you believe that everything happens for a reason, that includes what is perceived as both good and bad.
- Soul agreements were made to have specific lessons in this lifetime. Some of the most difficult experiences are the greatest gifts ... eventually.
- Oftentimes the value in the experience cannot be recognized until later (or in Spirit).

Points to Ponder
When you hear the phrase "everything happens for a reason", how do you feel?

_____

_____

_____

_____

_____

_____

_____

_____

_____

_____

_____

Lesson 7
Why Me?

Why do the same things happen over and over again? It's time to take personal responsibility instead of being a victim and/or blaming.

Key Takeaways

- You continue to manifest experiences in the same level of vibration that you stay in. Law of Attraction.
- If someone else is responsible for your experiences, then the power is always in their hands.
- Arguing for your limitations rather than empowering yourself to take the responsibility for change will keep you stuck in that experience.

Points to Ponder

Do you tend to identify with being a victim or being overly responsible? How can you maybe create more balance in your life?

_____

_____

_____

_____

_____

_____

_____

_____

_____

Lesson 8
Get Out of Your Head

Get out of your head and into your heart to set an intention, see the bigger picture, and create a new story.

Key Takeaways

- Put your hand on your heart and ask Spirit to help guide you toward a higher vibration and greater insight and awareness about this experience.
- Do a brain dump … to get out of your head and into your heart.
- Write about your new story. Empower yourself by creating a new story you want to tell.

Points to Ponder

Describe how you feel when you think about your new story:

_____

_____

_____

_____

_____

_____

_____

_____

_____

_____

Eyes Wide Open
Homework Action Items

Recognize the Purpose

- ☐ Visualize white light coming into your crown to create a Spirit connection so as to become more open to seeing messages and signs.
- ☐ Ask Spirit to show you a sign that they are with you.
- ☐ Pay attention to signs and symbols from Spirit throughout your day: Numbers, letters, words, symbols, songs, etc. Jot down the messages you catch.

Recognize Assistance from My Body

- ☐ Tune in when you have any physical manifestation (pain, sickness, or irritation) that shows up in your body ... describe the emotional energy you are in that may be causing it?
- ☐ Look up what the emotional foundation of the diseases or ailments that you may be experiencing are, and journal about how they may apply to you right now.
- ☐ Notice the impact that other's words or actions have on you and your body and what the message is behind them. (*What triggers you?*) List those and what they emotionally represent for you.

Own Responsibility for My Life

- ☐ Look at your environment around you and list everything you notice in your present space for the next 5 minutes.
- ☐ Think back thru the last 24 hours and write down all the internal and external judgements you are aware of that you felt.
- ☐ Make a list of who you blame for the challenges or difficulties in your life and why.

Create Something Different

- ☐ Become aware of what you are wanting or not wanting: List what is not working in your life and flip the words to the exact opposite to describe what you do want.
- ☐ Think about an old story you have been telling that you are sick and tired of owning, and tell it in a different way, with a positive spin on it.
- ☐ Think about one of the most difficult times in your life. Can you see now, in hindsight, how that exact thing happened for a reason? You may not like the reason, but can you see the value in it? Journal about your insights.

REMINDER: These Action Items can be done any time during this Step, in any order you are drawn to ... and certainly not all should be completed at once, to allow you an opportunity to fully integrate the new behaviors.

Eyes Wide Open
Affirmations to Move Forward

- ♥ I recognize that everything happens for a reason.
- ♥ I am willing to call a truce and end the war within my body.
- ♥ I am ready to own personal responsibility for my life.
- ♥ I am willing to do something different than I have been doing.

Quick reminder, friends: Part of the integration process for this Healing Journey is completing the experiential Homework included in this Workbook. Remember to do your homework for this Step. Have you completed it for previous Steps? All of it?? Sometimes, starting at the beginning ... getting back to basics ... can be very powerful in the healing journey.

ELEV8
your life.love

ch ch ch Choices

Step 3

STEP 3
Ch Ch Ch Choices

This is the third step in your journey.

This is where all the fun begins. You roll up your sleeves and realize that you are the creator of your life and your experiences.

You'll know you are in the *Ch Ch Ch Choices* step if:

- You find yourself thinking "Not one more time, will I _____."
- You know if you don't do something differently, then nothing is going to change
- You are no longer arguing for your limitations
- You are asking "What's for my highest good?"

Do you see yourself in any of this breakdown?

If so, you've probably experienced at least one of these emotions:

- Empowered
- Confused
- Responsible
- Pressured
- Determined

Feel familiar? If so ... you are making choices.

Let's get started with our Video Lessons for this Step:

1. **Creating Your Life**
2. **You Have Choices**
3. **Not Choosing is a Choice**
4. **Gaining Clarity**
5. **Not One More Time**
6. **Responding, Not Reacting**
7. **Create a New Story**
8. **Me First**

Lesson 1
Creating Your Life

You are in charge of creating your life, both career and personal. No one can create for you. You are the powerful creator of your reality.

Key Takeaways

- You cannot create for someone else; and only you can create experiences for you in this present moment.
- Create new routines that feel in alignment for you … e.g. Morning journaling, setting an intention for the day, pulling cards, writing out your goals for the day.
- Everything in business is personal – your current vibration affects all aspects of your life.

Points to Ponder
What do you want to create in the next week? Month? Year?

_____

_____

_____

_____

_____

_____

_____

_____

_____

_____

_____

_____

Lesson 2
You Have Choices

You have a choice; you are not a victim. Ask for help, receive support, and allow others in.

Key Takeaways

- The Universe is happening for you, not to you.
- A choice you can make is to ask for help – and being open and willing to receive it. Ask, allow, believe, receive.
- Believing eyes … importance of sharing with people who can help support your vision.

Points to Ponder
They ways that I resist/accept receiving help and support are:

_____

_____

_____

_____

_____

_____

_____

_____

_____

_____

_____

_____

_____

Lesson 3
Not Choosing is a Choice

Not choosing is still a choice; staying stuck is choosing to stay in the feeling of pain.

Key Takeaways

- Every situation has a multitude of choices that you can make – even if you don't like them all. There are usually 9 choices for each situation.
- Not choosing is a choice itself.
- The first step in shifting out of a painful experience is allowing yourself to make a choice to move toward something different ... Stepping into the unknown. You can always make a new choice.

Points to Ponder
In what situation in your life have you been not choosing? Are you ready to choose yet?

_____

_____

_____

_____

_____

_____

_____

_____

_____

_____

_____

_____

Lesson 4
Gaining Clarity

Gather information to make your choices: physically, mentally, emotionally, spiritually. You get to choose from a variety of sources based on your needs, wants, and desires.

Key Takeaways

- Examining your choices may require you to research more information about your situation so you have options that feel more in alignment for you, whether that is physically, mentally, emotionally, or spiritually.
- Allow yourself to choose based on your own needs and desires, not someone else's.
- Do not decide if you are not clear... listen to your heart.

Points to Ponder
In what area(s) in your life do you need clarity, and what can you do today to seek it?

_____

_____

_____

_____

_____

_____

_____

_____

_____

_____

_____

_____

Lesson 5
Not One More Time

Doing the same thing over and over again and expecting a different result is the description of insanity ... I will NOT continue the pattern that brought me here.

Key Takeaways

- If nothing in your experience changes, then the experience will not change. When you know better you do better.
- Love yourself enough to make a choice to honor yourself and change the pattern that has caused you pain. It's time to be your own BFF.
- Once you have identified the pattern that has kept you stuck in the pain, make a commitment to yourself that you will not accept that pattern: *Not One More Time.*

Points to Ponder
What is **your** *"NOT ONE MORE TIME"*?

_____

_____

_____

_____

_____

_____

_____

_____

_____

_____

_____

_____

Lesson 6
Responding, Not Reacting

Break your patterns at the subconscious level by learning to respond, rather than react.

Key Takeaways

- Become aware of your subconscious reactions that are triggered by your painful experiences. Subconscious vs. conscious.
- Projection vs. Reflection: The difference between reflecting and learning the patterns vs. projecting and blaming others for those patterns.
- Take a step back, put your hand on your heart and listen.
- Become aware of your buttons and how they are pushed. Create a new pattern for yourself by making a conscious choice about how you want to feel about that situation in the now.

Points to Ponder

When I react, I feel _____.

_____

_____

_____

_____

_____

_____

_____

_____

_____

_____

Lesson 7
Create a New Story

Fear is a choice. By releasing the fear, you can create a new story.

Key Takeaways

- Fear can be of value when we are tuned into our instinctive messages from within; but fear can be a reaction learned from our past as well. How we react to fear is also a choice.
- By choosing to replace our learned reactions to fear, we can create a new story that is in alignment with our Present Moment experience.
- When I notice my thoughts are beginning to feel heavy, unsupportive, judgmental, or from a place of lack … it's my indicator that I am moving away from my new story.

Points to Ponder

My greatest fears come from _____.

_____

_____

_____

_____

_____

_____

_____

_____

_____

_____

Lesson 8
Me First

You love yourself enough to choose YOU First!

Key Takeaways

- The only one who can choose for you is you! Put yourself on your LIST, EVERYDAY!
- You cannot give to anyone else what you do not have first for yourself. Talked about unconditional love and who you have it for… or not.
- To become your greatest self, you must be willing to love you MOST! I love me more!

Points to Ponder
In what way(s) can you show more love to yourself today?

_____

_____

_____

_____

_____

_____

_____

_____

_____

_____

_____

_____

Ch Ch Ch Choices
Homework Action Items

Be My Own Best Friend

- ☐ Affirm daily: "I HAVE CHOICES!"
- ☐ Put yourself at the top of your calendar today and do something joyful for yourself for 1 hour.
- ☐ Do one thing to improve your health today.

Receive Support

- ☐ Pick one area in your life where you feel like you have no choices, and list all the possible outcomes from that experience – dig deep and really look at all your options.
- ☐ Share 10 ways in which you argue for your limitations / make excuses for yourself.
- ☐ Reach out for help to someone or something outside of yourself.

Create a New Story

- ☐ Make a choice to step into a fear today and write about the experience before and afterwards.
- ☐ Write out an old pattern or story that you are willing to change and burn those pages, symbolically letting it go.
- ☐ Write out the new story you choose to tell going forward and put it in a sacred place.

Start a New Routine

- ☐ Set the intention every morning for 11 days to allow yourself the freedom to choose _____ (whatever is the most important choice point for you right now).
- ☐ Pick a new way to do something every day for a week: choose a different type of food to eat, drive a new way to work, listen to a different podcast or style of music (anything to break up typical habits).
- ☐ Select a new activity that supports and nurtures YOU and continue to do it for 21 days.

REMINDER: These Action Items can be done any time during this Step, in any order you are drawn to ... and certainly not all should be completed at once, to allow you an opportunity to fully integrate the new behaviors.

Ch Ch Ch Choices
Affirmations to Move Forward

- ♥ I accept and embrace my body as my BFF.
- ♥ I am open to receive support from other people and places.
- ♥ I am willing to step out of my fear and release the old patterns and create a new story.
- ♥ I am ready to commit to being consistent in a new habit for 21 days.

Quick reminder, friends: Part of the integration process for this Healing Journey is completing the experiential Homework included in this Workbook. Remember to do your homework for this Step. Have you completed it for previous Steps? All of it?? Sometimes, starting at the beginning ... getting back to basics ... can be very powerful in the healing journey.

ELEV8
yourlife.love

Lights!
Camera!
Action!

♡ Step 4

STEP 4
Lights!!! Camera!!! Action!!!

This is the fourth step in your journey.

This is where the movement starts picking up steam!

You'll know you are in the *Lights!!! Camera!!! Action!!!* step if:

- You make the shift from knowing to doing
- You struggle to follow through with your intentions
- You have a willingness to change
- You adopt a new health routine
- You are uneasy participating in new activities that support and nurture you
- You connect with like-minded people

Do you see yourself in any of this breakdown?

If so, you've probably experienced at least one of these emotions:

- Scared
- Uncertain
- Eager
- Empowered
- Uncomfortable

Feel familiar? If so ... you are taking action.

Let's get started with our Video Lessons for this Step:

1. **Put Yourself on the List**
2. **Manifest Anything You Desire**
3. **Vulnerability is the New Strength**
4. **Commitment & Consistency**
5. **Pushing thru the Fear**
6. **Take a Risk**
7. **Do Something Different**
8. **Be a Lighthouse**

Lesson 1
Put Yourself on the List

Put yourself on your list – literally! Do something for you each day.

Key Takeaways

- Use the example of the airplane: Put your mask on first, then help others.
- If you do not have time allotted for something for you on your calendar, it is only a dream, not a goal.
- Raising your vibration by doing something that brings you joy every day is the best way to begin your creation process.

Points to Ponder
When I put myself on the list I feel _____ .

_____

_____

_____

_____

_____

_____

_____

_____

_____

_____

_____

_____

Lesson 2
Manifest Anything You Desire

Manifestation is simply bringing things in to physical form.

Key Takeaways

- Manifestation in the physical world involves lining up your thoughts and feelings with that intention in your heart.
- You cannot create for someone else because you can't FEEL for someone else.
- Select something in your life that you want to put your attention/intention toward manifesting right now and follow the 6 Steps to Manifestation to begin that process today.
- A Vision board is a great way to manifest.

Points to Ponder
You are the creator of your reality ... what does that reality look like today?

_____

_____

_____

_____

_____

_____

_____

_____

_____

_____

_____

_____

Lesson 3
Vulnerability is the New Strength

Vulnerability is the new strength ... so get out of your box and share from an open and willing place.

Key Takeaways

- It takes courage to step out from the protective walls that have been created between yourself and others. Being vulnerable allows a new level of trust to be created within yourself and with others.
- Do something that scares you (in your head), but you know in your heart is safe for you to do.
- Taking an action that feels vulnerable creates new levels of connection and helps us to see we are more alike than different.

Points to Ponder
Vulnerability feels like:

_____

_____

_____

_____

_____

_____

_____

_____

_____

_____

_____

Lesson 4
Commitment & Consistency

Commitment and consistency ... and why they are the KEYS to healing.

Key Takeaways

- You must be accountable to yourself to maintain a commitment to yourself. The biggest commitment we will ever make is the one we make to ourselves.
- You must create a new habit for at least 21 days to allow that pattern to become consistent. Baby steps are just fine. Choose one thing to commit to right now.
- Commitment and consistency create the new patterns in your life that re-write the old painful stories. The more time you get under your belt, the more it becomes a habit.
- Accountability – that's why I am here ... that's what the mentoring time is for: To call you on your stuff and cheerlead you at the same time. Be sure to have someone in your life that does this for you.

Points to Ponder

There are areas of your life that you are likely extremely consistent and some, not so much. List a few of them and why.

_____

_____

_____

_____

_____

_____

_____

_____

_____

Lesson 5
Pushing thru the Fear

Stay in the present moment. Look at your past fears; explore how fear feels in the body.

Key Takeaways

- Fear is a natural emotion ... consider how many of its qualities feel similar to excitement in how it manifests in your body.
- "Thank you for sharing, I'm not interested, I'm choosing to focus on _____."
- Fears stored in the body can be brought up and out by writing them down and burning those pages to transmute the old energy.
- FEAR – False Evidence Appearing Real – Recognizing that it's through your stream of thoughts that it keeps the energy alive.

Points to Ponder

Fear is _____.

_____

_____

_____

_____

_____

_____

_____

_____

_____

_____

_____

Lesson 6
Take a Risk

Pick something that gives you some butterflies ... and take action from an inspired place.

Key Takeaways

- Empower yourself by choosing to do something that fear has held you back from doing in the past.
- Exposure therapy – the more you do it, the easier it gets.
- Listen for your guidance on what type of action you can be inspired to take from a place of love, not fear.
- Begin to experience the world as a safe place, one that is there to support you. Learning to trust the Universe.

Points to Ponder
As you think about taking a risk, what do you feel inside?

_____

_____

_____

_____

_____

_____

_____

_____

_____

_____

_____

Lesson 7
Do Something Different

Break those subconscious patterns by doing something different.

Key Takeaways

- By gaining awareness about what reactions are being triggered, it allows you to make new choices.
- Taking a different action disrupts that cycle.
- Don't allow the fear to keep you in the old story. When it shows up, change the story. Tell it the way you want to see it, in your own mind.
- What you wish others would do differently is likely what you wish you would do too. Look within to see if there is a critical voice at play.

Points to Ponder

If you were to take on a totally new behavior that is truly foreign to you – but gets you excited – what would it be?

_____

_____

_____

_____

_____

_____

_____

_____

_____

_____

Lesson 8
Be a Lighthouse

Connect with like-minds to give and receive support. We can all be a lighthouse for each other. Step into your purpose.

Key Takeaways

- As Beings of Unconditional Love, we were meant to connect in community with one another. Reach out in some way.
- The infinite cycle of giving and receiving allows that there are times when we shine the light for others during challenges; and there are times when others hold the light as we move forward.
- With the willingness to give and receive support in our like-minded community, we are serving our purpose in the Universe.
- Open your arms to the Universe, go out and face the sun and breathe the energy of receiving in.

Points to Ponder
In what way do you – or could you – shine your light for those around you?

_____

_____

_____

_____

_____

_____

_____

_____

_____

Lights!!! Camera!!! Action!!!
Homework Action Items

Feel in Harmony

- ☐ Call in your angels (Archangel Michael) to help hold your vibration/support your energy.
- ☐ Every day for a week, take 10 minutes in the morning and connect with a loved one in Spirit and ask them for a sign.
- ☐ Pick one way to improve your eating habits, sleeping habits, or exercise routine for one week … (select something to change in your physical world).

Be of Service

- ☐ Write down 5 changes that you want to make in your life and set one goal to make each one happen.
- ☐ After waking up in the morning, thank Spirit for this beautiful day and ask, *"How May I Be of Service?"* Listen throughout the day for your answer.
- ☐ Enroll in or complete a class or do a random act of kindness for a stranger.

Walk My Talk

- ☐ Ask your angels for inspired action and take it.
- ☐ Commit to sharing one personal affirmation per day via social media for 11 days.
- ☐ Post a video of something you are passionate about, preferably with you talking about it.

Share My Experiences

- ☐ Do something you are afraid of today.
- ☐ Post a 5-minute video of what success looks like to you.
- ☐ Reach out to a person that you know is struggling in a similar way as you have in the past. Share with them your experience and offer them some support, encouragement, or simply an ear to listen.

REMINDER: These Action Items can be done any time during this Step, in any order you are drawn to … and certainly not all should be completed at once, to allow you an opportunity to fully integrate the new behaviors.

Lights!!! Camera!!! Action!!!
Affirmations to Move Forward

- ♥ I feel in harmony with my mind, body, spirit, and emotions.
- ♥ I am ready to be of service to others.
- ♥ I am willing to walk my talk.
- ♥ I am open to sharing my experiences from a place of authenticity and vulnerability.

Quick reminder, friends: Part of the integration process for this Healing Journey is completing the experiential Homework included in this Workbook. Remember to do your homework for this Step. Have you completed it for previous Steps? All of it?? Sometimes, starting at the beginning ... getting back to basics ... can be very powerful in the healing journey.

ELEV8
yourlife.love

I'm Feelin' the Healin'

Step 5

STEP 5
I'm Feelin' the Healin'

This is the fifth step in your journey.

This is where you are making positive changes in your life and building up your feelings of confidence and gratitude!

You'll know you are in the *I'm Feelin' the Healin'* step if:

- You can recognize the value of your experiences
- You want to engage more and share more with others
- You know that you are moving forward
- You are frustrated that setbacks still occur
- You struggle to set healthy boundaries in your new world and awareness

Do you see yourself in any of this breakdown?

If so, you've probably experienced at least one of these emotions:

- Forgiveness
- Frustration
- Peace
- Inspiration
- Empowerment

Feel familiar? If so ... you are Feelin' the Healin'.

Let's get started with our Video Lessons for this Step:

1. **The Bigger Picture**
2. **Forgiveness**
3. **Taking your Energy Back**
4. **Filling Up**
5. **Bring the Joy**
6. **Maintaining a High Vibe**
7. **The 9-Step Process**
8. **Supporting Others**

Lesson 1
The Bigger Picture

The bigger picture becomes clear when you can see the gifts in the challenges – while you are still in it.

Key Takeaways

- Finding the value or seeing the purpose in an experience allows you to see the gifts in any experience … and stay open to receive them.
- Call in your Angels, specifically Archangel Uriel, to help you see the bigger picture.
- Seeing the bigger picture allows you to have more trust in the process that is taking place.

Points to Ponder
Focus on one of life's greatest challenges right now … what could be the bigger picture in it all?

_____

_____

_____

_____

_____

_____

_____

_____

_____

_____

_____

Lesson 2
Forgiveness

Forgive yourself and others. Ask for help from Spirit to truly forgive ... How do you know when you have really forgiven?

Key Takeaways

- Sometimes we are the teacher, sometimes we are the student ~ regardless of the relationship. Finding the value in a situation can lead you to true forgiveness of yourself or others that were involved in that situation.
- Viewing a past experience with appreciation and insight to the bigger picture is the key to arriving at true forgiveness.
- Ask Archangel Zadkiel to assist you in finding true forgiveness of yourself or others in any situation.

Points to Ponder

My greatest teachers have taught me _____.

_____

_____

_____

_____

_____

_____

_____

_____

_____

_____

Lesson 3
Taking your Energy Back

Reclaim your energy from anyone you have given it away to. Visualize restoring your energy field and taking your power back.

Key Takeaways

- No one can make you feel a certain way without your permission.
- In past situations, you may not have maintained healthy energy boundaries with other individuals.
- You can reclaim your energy now using a visualization process to call back your own energy to yourself.
- Take your power back in your relationships by restoring your own energy field and maintain your energy by observing – not absorbing – energy going forward.

Points to Ponder
Sometimes I give my power away by _____.

_____

_____

_____

_____

_____

_____

_____

_____

_____

_____

Lesson 4
Filling Up

Understand your value and don't give away too much of yourself. Allow more abundance/energy into your life. Find the harmony in all you do.

Key Takeaways

- Creating space to fill yourself up is just as important as the level of giving that you do. What will you do for Joy today?
- The harmony (as opposed to balance) in this energy exchange allows for more energy to flow into your life without giving too much of yourself away.
- Abundance is a form of energy. The allowing in of this energy creates opportunity for more giving of that energy too.
- When you release yucky energy, it must be replaced with a higher vibration of energy ... or the same energy you released will find its way back quickly.

Points to Ponder
It is easiest for me to fill up when I _____.

_____

_____

_____

_____

_____

_____

_____

_____

_____

_____

Lesson 5
Bring the Joy

Choose to generate the energy of joy in everything you experience.

Key Takeaways

- You are responsible for your own happiness. No one else can be responsible for your happiness ... that is a dead-end road.
- No matter what task you are doing, you can bring the energy of joy into that moment. We are generators of energy.
- Your positive energy and outlook can improve, simply by the Law of Attraction, any situation you are in.

Points to Ponder
What does true joy look like to you?

_____

_____

_____

_____

_____

_____

_____

_____

_____

_____

_____

Lesson 6
Maintaining a High Vibe

Be consistent in maintaining a high vibe daily. Be accountable to yourself.

Key Takeaways

- Create a routine that allows you to create from a higher vibration every day. Begin with meditation.
- Connect with nature. Let Her support your energy.
- Use affirmations or mantras throughout your day.
- Surround yourself with high vibe people and community.

Points to Ponder
List ways that you can bring that high vibe energy in:

_____

_____

_____

_____

_____

_____

_____

_____

_____

_____

_____

_____

_____

Lesson 7
The 9-Step Process

Use the 9-Step process from Awareness to Appreciation to find the value in every experience.

Key Takeaways

- Select a challenge that you wish to find a greater value for in that experience.
- Use the 9-Step Process Worksheet to move from Awareness to Appreciation of some aspect of that situation.
- Take some action to lock in a new understanding of the purpose in that experience for yourself.

Points to Ponder

What I discovered in the 9-Step Process is _____.

_____

_____

_____

_____

_____

_____

_____

_____

_____

_____

_____

_____

Lesson 8
Supporting Others

We teach what we need to learn. Shine your Light and share it with others.

Key Takeaways

- As Beings of Unconditional Love, we are here to support each other in this human experience.
- Do a random act of kindness.
- No one has the unique collection of gifts that you have to shine out into the world. Be your Authentic Self. Share a message of love from your heart with someone today.
- Being of service and sharing those gifts with others is often the best way to focus on those areas of our own life that we are meant to continue to grow and expand in as well. Is there someone you know could use a little boost? Offer them a hand or a shoulder.

Points to Ponder

There are so many ways to be of service ... List a few of your favorites and then get out there and do them.

_____

_____

_____

_____

_____

_____

_____

_____

_____

I'm Feelin' the Healin'
Homework Action Items

Maintain Energy

- ☐ Share a picture of a calendar with YOUR time blocked off on it.
- ☐ Do something that brings you joy every day for one week.
- ☐ Visualize taking your energy back from someone you gave it away to previously.
- ☐ Write 33 things you appreciate about your past and present.

Use Your Tools

- ☐ Identify the tools you use to stay connected in mind, body, and spirit ... and list your top 5 tools most active right now.
- ☐ Write a letter of forgiveness (to yourself or someone else) and burn it; then remember to do something to fill up.
- ☐ Choose someone to support or encourage for the next week ... without explanation or telling them that it's a project ... and connect with them as guided by your heart throughout the week.
- ☐ Share a recent experience where you were able to respond, instead of reacting.

Grow & Expand

- ☐ List 10 things you are inspired by or inspired to do – pick one to reach out for, engage in, donate to, or take action around.
- ☐ Think of one of the most difficult experiences of your life and share within our community what you feel is the value/purpose of it.
- ☐ Share a message that requires you to be vulnerable and open on social media. It will feel a bit risky, but not over the top.
- ☐ Write down your three biggest goals and share the steps you WILL take to get there.

REMINDER: These Action Items can be done any time during this Step, in any order you are drawn to ... and certainly not all should be completed at once, to allow you an opportunity to fully integrate the new behaviors.

I'm Feelin' the Healin'
Affirmations to Move Forward

- ♥ I live my life joyfully.
- ♥ I am sharing my authentic self.
- ♥ I am of service to others.
- ♥ I am open and willing to receive all the abundance and love that life has to offer.

Quick reminder, friends: Part of the integration process for this Healing Journey is completing the experiential Homework included in this Workbook. Remember to do your homework for this Step. Have you completed it for previous Steps? All of it?? Sometimes, starting at the beginning ... getting back to basics ... can be very powerful in the healing journey.

ABOUT THE AUTHOR

Sunny Dawn Johnston is a world-renowned inspirational speaker, spiritual teacher, and psychic medium. She's the author of twenty books, including her two flagship bestsellers, *Invoking the Archangels* and *The Love Never Ends*, which have become the cornerstones for many of her keynote topics such as intuition, mediumship, and the angelic realm.

Sunny's community of devoted clients and students expands the globe, and through her courses, private sessions, and live events, Sunny has touched the lives of thousands, both online and in-person. Her clients best know Sunny for her infinite, unconditional love and lack of judgment as she prides herself on always coming from a place of integrity, both in life and in her work.

Sunny helps people **connect with their heart** and **release the things that hold them back** from being their greatest version of themselves. Combining the *unconditional love* of a mother and the *tell-it-like-it-is honesty* of a best friend, Sunny helps people move into a higher vibration of living ... *and* a higher vibration of **Being**. Using her spiritual and intuitive gifts, she shines a light on the areas of lack, fear, insecurity and sometimes ... *B***S***!* Sunny feels strongly that at the heart of these issues is a lack of *Self-Love*. By reflecting the **true nature** of her clients back to them – **which *IS* Love** – they can experience, and then allow in that unconditional love, and begin to heal themselves.

Sunny's latest endeavor, **SDJ Productions,** has expanded her beyond writing and speaking events and into publishing and producing. Her latest projects include two multi-author compilations, **365 Days of Angel Prayers** and **111 Morning Meditations,** with many more in the works.

In her spare time, Sunny is actively involved in the spiritual community and volunteers as a psychic investigator for the international organization **FIND ME**. This is a not-for-profit organization of Psychic, Investigative, and Canine Search & Rescue (SAR) volunteers working together to provide leads to law enforcement and families of missing persons and homicide.

Sunny resides in Glendale, Arizona surrounded by a loving family and close friends. She believes in maintaining a healthy mix of work and play and encourages harmony in all areas of life.

To learn more about Sunny's work, please **visit her website:**
www.sunnydawnjohnston.com

And connect with her in her **private Facebook group:**
www.facebook.com/groups/SDJCommunity.

Additionally, Sunny invites you to join her virtual community *ELEV8 Your Life*, a membership site where you'll gain access to her 5-step healing process based on her 18 years of teaching, including her online courses and all her best content. www.elev8yourlife.love

Made in United States
North Haven, CT
03 September 2022

23615255R00046